Contents

Here is a honeybee.

A honeybee is an insect. This means that it has six legs, a pair of wings and two eyes. Bees live together in large groups called **colonies**.

Watch It Grow

Bee

Barrie Watts

W

FRANKLIN WATTS
LONDON • SYDNEY

This edition 2008

Franklin Watts
338 Euston Road, London NW1 3BH

Franklin Watts Australia
Level 17/207 Kent Street, Sydney, NSW 2000

Editor: Kate Newport
Art director: Jonathan Hair
Photographer: Barrie Watts
Illustrator: David Burroughs

The author would like to thank Steve Porter for his invaluable help
and assistance in the preparation of this book.

A CIP catalogue record for this book
is available from the British Library

ISBN 978 0 7496 8296 5

Printed in China

How to use this book

Watch It Grow has been specially designed to cater for a
range of reading and learning abilities. Initially children may
just follow the pictures. Ask them to describe in their own
words what they see. Other children will enjoy reading the
single sentence in large type, in conjunction with the pictures.
This single sentence is then expanded in the main text. More
adept readers will be able to follow the text and pictures by
themselves through to the conclusion of the life cycle.

Franklin Watts is a division of Hachette Children's Books, an Hachette Livre UK company.

People often keep bees in bee **hives** to
collect the **honey** they make. There
can be as many as 50,000 bees living
in a hive. In the wild, bees make their
homes in hollow trees.

The queen bee lays eggs.

Each **colony** of bees has a **queen bee**. She is the only bee to lay eggs. She lays each one in a different **cell** of the wax **honeycomb** that makes up the **hive**.

The other bees in the hive fall into two groups: female workers and male **drones**. The **worker bees** make the honeycomb wax. It comes from four **glands** under their stomach.

The egg is small.

The bee egg is very small, about the size of a pinhead. The **queen bee** lays most of her eggs during the warm weather. She lays up to 3,000 eggs each day.

She carefully glues each egg to the bottom of a **cell.** As soon as it is laid, the egg starts to change. Inside, a bee **larva** is growing.

The egg hatches.

After three days, the egg hatches
and a bee **larva** crawls out. The
larva is creamy-white and about
as long as a grain of rice.
It looks like a small maggot.

The **worker bees** start feeding it a liquid food called **royal jelly**. When the larva is small, it floats in the **cell** on a pool of royal jelly. Larvae hatch out all the time, so they are all different sizes in the cells.

The worker bees feed the larvae.

The younger **worker bees**, called **house bees**, look after the **hive**. They take care of the queen and her eggs, and feed the **larvae**.

There can be as many as 10,000 larvae growing in a large hive. The house bees must keep the larvae supplied with food as new bees are needed to work in the hive.

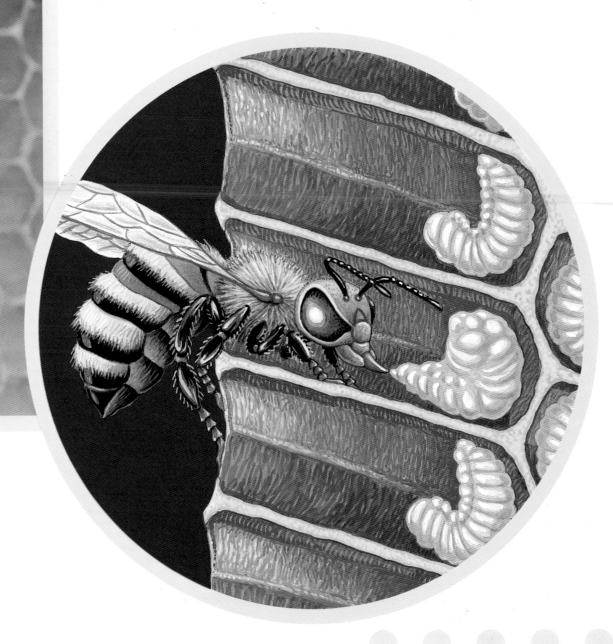

The larva grows.

On the fourth day, the **worker bees** stop feeding the **larva royal jelly**. Instead, they feed the larva on **pollen** and **honey**.

The workers look after the larva very well and feed it over 1,000 times every day. As the larva grows, it sheds its skin, just like a butterfly caterpillar. It does this five times in its life as a larva.

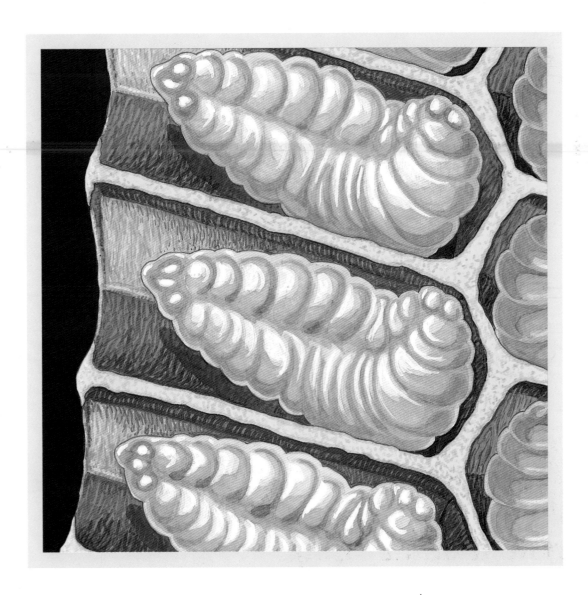

The workers seal the cell.

Eight days after hatching, the **larva** is fully grown and fills the **cell**. It is now so big it cannot curl up. Its mouth is facing the cell entrance.

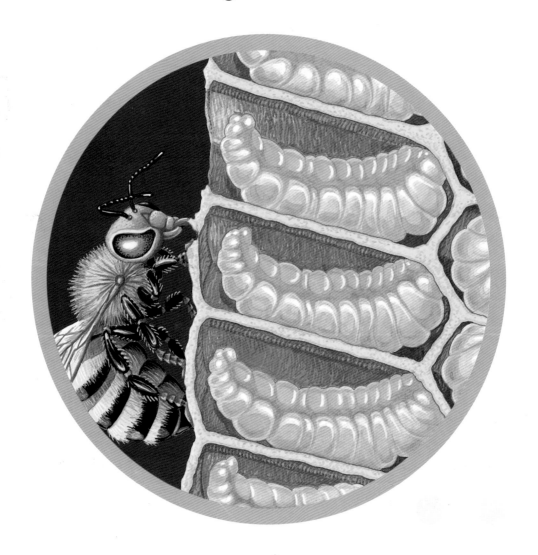

The workers stop feeding the larva and put a cap of wax on the cell to seal it. The cap lets air through so the larva can breathe.

The larva turns into a pupa.

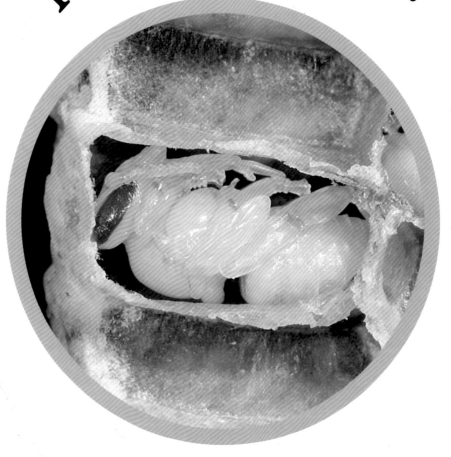

The **larva** cannot feed anymore and it starts to change into a **pupa**. Three days after the **cell** has been capped, the larva sheds its skin for the last time.

Underneath is a pupa. It looks like a bee without wings. But beneath its soft skin the pupa is changing into a fully-grown bee.

The bee emerges.

After nine days the **pupa** changes
colour. It has turned into an adult
bee inside the pupa case. Its eyes
are dark and its wings have grown.

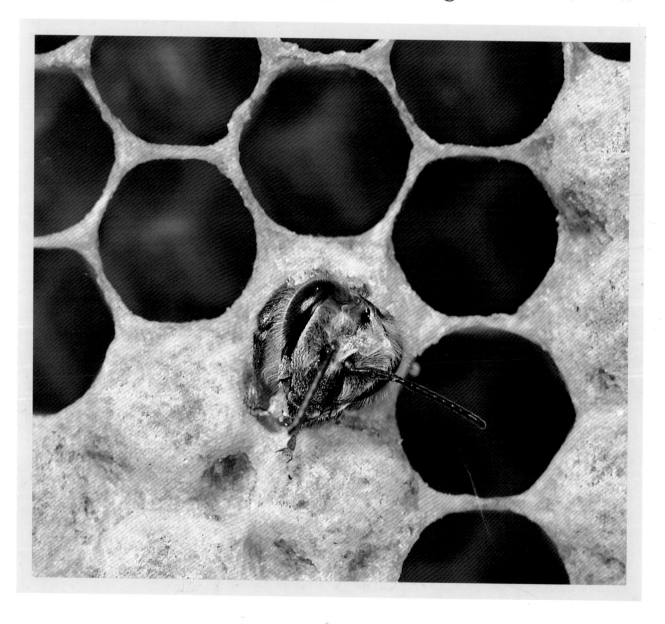

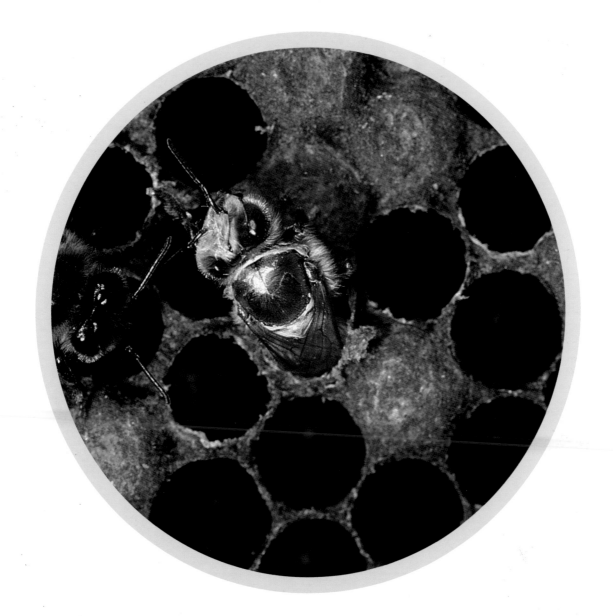

It chews its way through the cap and struggles out of the **cell**, leaving the old pupa case behind. At first, the bee's body is soft and its wings are crumpled. After a day the body hardens and the bee can fly.

The bee leaves the hive.

The **worker bee** has a job to do. In the summer, worker bees only live for about six weeks. For the first two weeks, the bee will work in the **hive** cleaning out the **cells** and looking after the queen and the **drones**.

When it is about three or four weeks old, the bee will leave the hive to find **pollen** and **nectar** in flowers. Other bees tell it where to go by dancing in front of it.

The bee finds food.

Bees are busy among the flowers on warm sunny days. Flying from plant to plant uses up a lot of energy, so a **worker bee** will feed on **honey** before it leaves the **hive**.

A worker bee collects **pollen** and **nectar** from flowers and takes it to the hive. It also carries pollen from one flower to another. This pollinates the flower so it can form its seeds.

The bee stores the food.

The bees keep the **nectar** they collect in a special stomach. When their honey stomach is full, they return home and give the nectar and the **pollen** to the **house bees**.

The house bees then chew the nectar and turn it into **honey**. They store the new honey and fresh pollen in empty **honeycomb cells**. When each cell is full, they seal it with wax.

The workers feed the queen.

The **worker bees** feed the **queen bee** all the time so she can carry on laying eggs. She only lives for about two to three years. As she gets older, she lays fewer eggs. When this happens, the workers select a **larva** and feed it extra **royal jelly**. This larva will become the **hive's** next queen.

Word bank

Cells - Small round spaces in the honeycomb where the queen bee places the eggs after they are laid.

Colonies - When living things live together in large groups it is called a colony.

Drones - Male bees who rely on the labour of the worker bees.

Glands - Parts of an animal's body that give out a substance. Worker bees have glands that give out wax.

Hives - A house for bees that makes it easy to collect honey. In the wild, bees have nests in hollow trees.

Honey - A sweet, thick fluid produced by bees from the nectar of flowers.

Honeycomb - Groups of cells made of wax where bees store their honey and raise their young.

House bees - Younger worker bees who look after the hive and take care of the queen and feed the larvae.

Larvae - After bees hatch, they live as bee larvae until they grow their skin and wings. Larvae look like maggots.

Nectar -A sweet sugary liquid that attracts bees to flowers. Bees make honey from nectar.

Queen bee - The only bee that lays eggs.

Pollen - A fine yellow powder that is produced by male flowers.

Pupa - The stage an insect goes through as it changes from larva to adult.

Royal jelly - A rich liquid food that the worker bees feed to the larva.

Worker bees - The female bees that produce the wax, run the hive and take care of the larvae.

Life cycle

The queen lays each egg in a different cell of the honeycomb.

When it is about three or four weeks old, the bee will leave the hive.

As soon as the egg is laid, a bee larva is growing inside it.

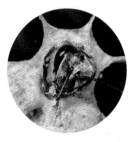

After nine days the pupa changes colour. It has turned into an adult.

After three days, the egg hatches and a larva crawls out.

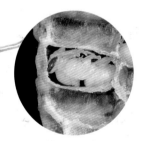

The larva cannot feed anymore and it starts to change into a pupa.

As the larva grows, it sheds its skin. It does this five times.

Eight days after hatching, the bee larva is fully grown.

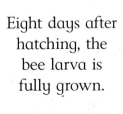

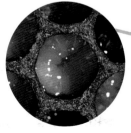

Index